WEDDING PLANNER AND ORGANIZERS 2019

CALENDAR

JANUARY

FEBRUARY

MARCH

APRIL

MAY

JUNE

JULY

AUGUST

SEPTEMBER

OCTOBER

NOVEMBER

DECEMBER

BUDGET WORKSHEET

WEDDING BUDGET	BUDGET	ACTUAL
	$	$
	$	$
	$	$
	$	$
	$	$
	$	$
	$	$
	$	$
	$	$
	$	$
	$	$
	$	$
	$	$
	$	$
	$	$
	$	$
	$	$
	$	$
	$	$
	$	$
	$	$
SUBTOTAL	$	$
GRAND TOTAL	$	$

GUEST LIST WORKSHEET

LIST OF NAMES	INVITE SENT	TABLE NUMBER	THANK YOU SENT

GUEST LIST WORKSHEET

LIST OF NAMES	INVITE SENT	TABLE NUMBER	THANK YOU SENT

GUEST LIST WORKSHEET

LIST OF NAMES	INVITE SENT	TABLE NUMBER	THANK YOU SENT

GUEST LIST WORKSHEET

LIST OF NAMES	INVITE SENT	TABLE NUMBER	THANK YOU SENT

GUEST LIST WORKSHEET

LIST OF NAMES	INVITE SENT	TABLE NUMBER	THANK YOU SENT

GUEST LIST WORKSHEET

LIST OF NAMES	INVITE SENT	TABLE NUMBER	THANK YOU SENT

GUEST LIST WORKSHEET

LIST OF NAMES	INVITE SENT	TABLE NUMBER	THANK YOU SENT

GUEST LIST WORKSHEET

LIST OF NAMES	INVITE SENT	TABLE NUMBER	THANK YOU SENT

CHECK LIST

- [ ]
- [ ]
- [ ]
- [ ]
- [ ]
- [ ]
- [ ]
- [ ]
- [ ]
- [ ]
- [ ]
- [ ]
- [ ]
- [ ]
- [ ]
- [ ]
- [ ]
- [ ]
- [ ]
- [ ]
- [ ]
- [ ]
- [ ]
- [ ]
- [ ]
- [ ]
- [ ]
- [ ]
- [ ]
- [ ]

CHECK LIST

- [ ]
- [ ]
- [ ]
- [ ]
- [ ]
- [ ]
- [ ]
- [ ]
- [ ]
- [ ]
- [ ]
- [ ]
- [ ]
- [ ]
- [ ]
- [ ]
- [ ]
- [ ]
- [ ]
- [ ]
- [ ]
- [ ]
- [ ]
- [ ]
- [ ]
- [ ]
- [ ]
- [ ]
- [ ]

CHECK LIST

CHECK LIST

- ☐
- ☐
- ☐
- ☐
- ☐
- ☐
- ☐
- ☐
- ☐
- ☐
- ☐
- ☐
- ☐
- ☐
- ☐
- ☐
- ☐
- ☐
- ☐
- ☐
- ☐
- ☐
- ☐
- ☐
- ☐
- ☐
- ☐
- ☐
- ☐
- ☐

NOTES

NOTES

NOTES

NOTES

NOTES

NOTES

NOTES

NOTES

NOTES

NOTES

NOTES

NOTES

NOTES

NOTES

NOTES

NOTES

NOTES

NOTES

NOTES

NOTES

NOTES

NOTES

NOTES

NOTES

NOTES

NOTES

NOTES

NOTES

NOTES

NOTES

NOTES

NOTES

NOTES

NOTES

NOTES

NOTES

NOTES

NOTES

NOTES

NOTES

NOTES

NOTES

NOTES

NOTES

NOTES

NOTES

NOTES

NOTES

NOTES

NOTES

NOTES

NOTES

NOTES

NOTES

NOTES

NOTES

NOTES

NOTES

NOTES

NOTES

NOTES

NOTES

NOTES

NOTES

NOTES

NOTES

NOTES

NOTES

NOTES

NOTES

NOTES

NOTES

NOTES

NOTES

NOTES

NOTES

NOTES

NOTES

NOTES

NOTES

NOTES

NOTES

NOTES

NOTES

NOTES

NOTES

NOTES

NOTES

NOTES

NOTES

www.ingramcontent.com/pod-product-compliance
Lightning Source LLC
LaVergne TN
LVHW082249150826
845677LV00009B/1573

* 9 7 9 8 8 6 9 4 5 5 0 6 2 *